# SAFFRON TEA

The Heaventree Press

in association with **sampad**

# SAFFRON TEA

*edited by*
Kampta Karran
&
George Tolis

The Heaventree Press
in association with **sampad**

SAFFRON TEA

First edition 2003



Selection and Introduction



ISBN 0-9545317-1-X

The front cover painting is Untitled, acrylic on canvas, by Dilwara Begum ©2002.
The back cover photograph is of a textile from a collection titled *Memory Vessels,* manmade and natural yarns, by Dilwara Begum ©2003.
Both reproduced with permission.

Cover design by Dave Walsh and © **sampad** 2003.

Printed by Lydon Print, Birmingham.

*Published by*

The Heaventree Press

PO Box 3342

Coventry

CV1 5YB

England

*in association with* **sampad**

## CONTENTS

**Amina Shelly**



**Kalpana Ganguly**



**Kampta Karran**

## ACKNOWLEDGEMENTS

The production of an anthology of poetry is a collective endeavour, with so many helpers and well-wishers that it would be impossible to name them all. However, in the acknowledgement of debt, our poets, for making poetry, participating in meetings and workshops and for writing and rewriting their work, have earned our heartfelt gratitude. The people behind the scenes like Anouk Perinpanayagam, Kavita Bhanot and Anne Cockitt at sampad made sterling contributions that deserve much praise. The editors are also grateful to sampad for generously providing funding to sustain the project and produce the book. Finally, to Jon Morley and the Heaventree collective, for all their hard work, we say shukriya, thank you.

**sampad** is pleased to have been able to support the publication of Saffron Tea as part of its continuing commitment to develop, nurture and create new opportunities for British Asian writing throughout the West Midlands region.

## INTRODUCTION

An exploration of the origins of the poets in Saffron Tea takes us to India, Pakistan, Bangladesh, Kenya, Uganda, Tanzania, Guyana and the United Kingdom. It tells us of the long and chequered history of the interaction between the empire and the jewel in the crown. It is an experience of the crossing of boundaries, the myth of returning, the emergence of individual and collective ways of knowing and, ultimately, the search for permanent homes.

Any communion between civilisations demands that the issue of language be addressed. While the mother tongues of our contributors may be Sanskrit, Hindu or Urdu, this anthology uses English as its meeting point. Is this hegemony at work? Or is it the process of hybridisation? The answer lies in the philosophy of the reader.

The late Edward Said, described the effects of two cultures meeting on unequal footings: the dominant nation constructs the identity of the weaker in its own image, through language, customs and force. And yet the balance can be addressed: today those once written about are writing themselves. In this anthology, the writers value their experiences in words; they join the process of transforming the people of the South Asian Diaspora from merely objects of literature, to its subjects and creators.

Yesterday's migrants from the outposts of Empire are today's citizens of the emerging multicultural enterprise. There is no valid contradiction in being British and Asian at the same time. This book resonates with the influences of Tagore on the one hand and Kipling on the other. Saraswati, the Hindu Goddess of music and the arts stands alongside Jesus Christ, the son of the Christian God. Childhood memories of rural Bangladesh, struggles in postcolonial Guyana and Pakistan and the strain of metropolitan England are all elements through which this odyssey forges.

Saffron Tea is not just a contribution to the poetry of the South Asian Diaspora in Britain. Rather it is a celebration of our cosmopolitan heritage. Although the poems spring from diverse muses and unfold in a variety of forms, they tell a story that is integral to the larger national narrative. The reader is now invited to examine the collection and to form her or his critical appreciation.

KK & GT
*22nd October 2003*

## Asif Ahmed

Brought up and educated in London, Asif now lives in Birmingham, working as a Professor of Reproductive Physiology at the University of Birmingham. He has won two awards for poetry in America. His work has previously been published by The Cannon Poets, appearing in *Broadside XI* and also features on the Internet at www.englishpoets.com.

**Poetry Speaks…**

*Poetry speaks with an unedited tongue,*
*It warms the old, woos the young,*
*It frees the spirit, uplifts the mind,*
*It colours the world for the colour blind.*

## Saffron Tea

She is saffron tea to me
reborn from the funeral pyre
she is the history of the free
her songs set ice on fire

She is the salt on my lips
a symbol of the "Just Fight"
she is cool as swinging hips
sylvan as the setting light

She is the magic of May
like the first desert shower
she is the unexplored way
a rosebud yet to flower

She is the counsel of my cries
a torch to tease the dark away
she is the sunshine in my eyes
a glow to warm this cold clay

My pulse misses a heartbeat
as she walks carefree my way
hearts rejoice as lovers meet
and brighten the saffron day

**Harmony**

one day
down and dreaming
look out of my window
and
see
the dance of trees
leaves flicker like candlelight
branches swerve and swing
the woods rock n roll
under a saffron sun

and I remember
as a child I was told
never to go in the woods
alone, never alone

yet I see
pine kiss sycamore
oak caress elm
silver birch hug ash
and I hear
weeping willow
whisper have no fear
woods are your school

## Pillow Talk

As first light greets
each dawn I hear tip-tap of tiny feet,
worn-out wooden floors creak
as you sneak into my bed
for a pillow talk.

You sparkle like an effervescent drink
while I groan like a muffled drum.
You're soft as snow yet warm as mink,
while I am drowsy like Jamaican rum.

As we lay head-to-head in bed
with a smile of silk you simply said:
*Where is my bottle of milk?*

## Beyond the Blue

Let us go beyond the cold blue snow
our lives to catch the saffron day
make a bed of bluebells for our foe.

The Christ child had an eternal glow
three wise men knew this and they say
let us go beyond the cold blue snow.

Pull away the heavy cloak of woe
see the smiles spread this way
make a bed of bluebells for our foe.

As rivers of rainbows start to flow
hear the symphony of children's play
let us go beyond the cold blue snow.

Roll red lava into balls of snow
time to join our broken hands of clay
make a bed of bluebells for our foe.

And we my friends have seeds to sow
refuse the hangman's glove and say
let us go beyond the cold blue snow
make a bed of bluebells for our foe.

## The Soldier's Song

The horrors of war are like fine art
painted on life's erroneous scroll.
You sing hymns on my grave
and glory makes you blind.

*I lost my heart, I lost my soul,*
*I lost my limbs, I lost my mind,*
*I lost my love, I lost my friend.*

I was once a turtle dove,
now my conscience is my country.
She brings me peace and victory.

*I lost my heart, I lost my soul,*
*I lost my limbs, I lost my mind,*
*I lost my love, I lost my friend.*

I shall teach my child to hate all guns.
I shall teach myself the love of peace;
teach our sons to comprehend:

*I lost my heart, I lost my soul, I lost my limbs,*
*I lost my mind, I lost my love, I lost my friend.*

## "Truth is mocked and truth is halted"

when our government conspires
with the tyrants and dictators
flags of freedom fail to flutter
democracy melts like hot butter
justice is buried in the sand
humanity stretched like rubber band.

## Common Sense

Though her body radiates heat
she severs the CNS
with her "mind over matter" speech
nothing seems any more
to reach her heartbeat.

Her handbag is full of hang-ups
conventions clutter her synaptic connections.
Emotions are drying
like skirts on washing lines.

Note: CNS - Central Nervous System

## Beyond the Farmhouse

Heat has dulled the midday,
silver sun scorches our skin
as we make our weary way
back to the old farmhouse.

We pass strings of scarecrows
on crucifixes in the yellow grass.
Cut hay fills our lungs

as we enter the farmyard;
we welcome the shelter
and the shade. Beyond the field
the hills are glowing.

At dawn they are far away;
come dusk they swell and form
the very walls of our home.

**If You—**

If you simply live for pleasure,
are accumulating treasure
and inspire no one you touch,
have you done so very much?

If you despise social justice,
are not incensed by injustice,
or cries of help you will not hear,
can your conscience still be clear?

If your fibres will not forgive
pain and torture you make us relive
and revenge sets your rages free,
can you give way to a mercy plea?

If fanatics grow – you graze as sheep,
fascism reigns – you calmly sleep,
failing to grasp the hate campaign,
why weep when they inflict pain?

If the words you speak lack truth,
fooling the wise and trusting youth
and indifference is your only ration,
can you ever feel love's passion?

If you happily exploit the weak,
his just earnings you falsely keep,
failing to comprehend fair-play,
can you be our 'hand of clay'?

If you twist the words of a sage,
capturing with wealth the world stage
and let profit dictate your actions,
why then dismay at our reactions?

If you poison the mind of the people,
silencing the bells in the steeple,
clawing dawn into a Cimmerian night,
can you ever be our anchor light?

If your heartbeats cannot weep,
teeming minds stay fast asleep
and bright blue eyes fail to see
what hope have you to be?

**All you Need to Know**

At
every
start of day
blades of summer
bake trees into a host of chlorophyll.
Flowers are a challenge as the night sky
like the clean air
in still rooms
death comes.
We
shall sleep
in pure ease
like two bed sheets
boneless wisdom tinged with dull pink.

# Debjani Chatterjee

Debjani Chatterjee has written, translated and edited thirty books of poetry and prose for children and adults, as well as writing for the stage. She runs writing workshops around the country, for all ages. Her award-winning anthologies include *Barbed Lines* and *The Redbeck Anthology of British South Asian Poetry.*

**Swanning In**

Saraswati, you come swanning in, smooth
as ever on your gliding bird, playing
your goddess self and expect me to rise
          and honour you.

An unexpected guest, you never knock
at my mind's door. You fly in with élan
and chat like it was yesterday. Any
          window will do.

This is no neighbourhood in India,
nor is this Heaven, but you are at home
no matter where; folding white wings – your bird
          swans into view.

While great Brahma rests, you are the blossom
on his six eyes, his heart-strumming music.
But each polyglot lilt you sing to me
          has an echo

that belongs to your raucous bird. "Beauty,"
it winks, "has an ugly voice, serpentine
like my neck." Your company has a price,
          so I bow low

and make the most of any arrival.
Lady, I would put aside life itself,
if you would understand my need to hold
          when you let go.

Saraswati, you do not see the glint
in your bird's slanted eyes – a mortal dart.
Cushioned on airy clouds, impregnable,
you breathe incense.

Even in Fortress Britain where I draw
my mind's portcullis and double glaze all
windowpanes, you surprise me with your sudden
gracious presence.

Ringing the alarm about intruders
would have no effect. By the time help came
you would be long gone; a few swan feathers
for tantalising evidence.

Note: Saraswati, wife of Brahma the Creator, is the Goddess of Music and the Arts. The swan is her symbol.

## Watching the Male Mute

A found poem on reading
*Birdwatching on Inland Fresh Waters*, by M.A. Ogilvie

The resident and very tame Mute Swan
adopts a firm line with his offspring.

Few birds are more aggressive
in defence of their young,
neck feathers flared in furious display,
charging red-eyed over the water with wings
outstretched, feet flapping the surface,
soundly slapping the elements.

Late Autumn, all this changes.

On lake or gravel pit
the male Mute may be seen
defending territory
against all comers.
The cygnets too are now intruders.
He vigorously chases
until they are driven well away.
Singly or together,
dispatch them he will.

Such parental aggression can cause
some spectators a certain measure of distress:
it does rather seem as if he is striving
to kill his own young just days
after safeguarding them.

But it is a natural part of the swan's life.
The Mute Swan's method of sending
offspring out into the wide world
appears to work.

## Bahadur Shah Zafar

For Basir Sultan Kazmi

But two yards of land were all you wanted.
Your blind eyes shed tears for your motherland,
every inch of her soil was sacred.

"Hindustan's last emperor," they taunted,
"where are they now, the Mughals – great and grand?"
But two yards of land were all you wanted.

The slaughter of your princes was flaunted,
martyred blood flooded the Yamuna's sand.
Every inch of her soil was sacred.

Dead eyes gazed from Delhi gates, tormented.
History has noted their desperate stand.
But two yards of land were all you wanted.

The Dwarf had taken three steps undaunted;
Chittagong was claimed when holy flames fanned.
Every inch of her soil was sacred.

Your shattered heart and poetry pleaded,
yet your grave was dug in a foreign land.
But two yards of land were all you wanted,
every inch of her soil was sacred.

Note: The First War of Indian Independence (1857) was fought in the name of the poet-emperor Bahadur Shah Zafar (d. 1863). Two sons and a grandson had their heads displayed on a Delhi gate – now called *Khooni Darwaza* (Bloody Gate). Other royal males were also killed and the emperor exiled to Rangoon. Granted three steps of land, Vishnu's Dwarf avatar took Earth, Heaven and Hell. A Sufi saint wrested Chittagong from demons by asking for as much land as would be lit by his lamp.

## Our Lady of the Wayside Grotto

Your robe's cerulean folds
don't flutter in the wind,

but are lifted to wipe
the squirrel's whiskered face

as it washes itself –
a splash of red on blue.

The tilt of your draped head
speaks of modest prayer;

it rests the lone magpie
that remembers its mate

too loved this shrub-edged haunt –
black and white, life and death.

Your arms, spread in a wide
embrace of city air,

drip dewdrop blessings on
a mushrooming coppice

that guards your sacred space
in a wayside grotto.

Lady, the grass that grows
at your hidden feet sings

each season's hosannas
yards from the tarmac road

and bluebells peal praises
that ring endlessly true.

Our Lady, full of grace,
stand vigil by our world.

## Reason for Coming

For Nadia and Abdullah

"We had to come to Britain for our son;
        more can be done for him here,"
you said. Your role was simply caring.

Now Sheffield holds his eight years' bones
        and you are still in thrall, grieving.

## Sky

The sun is a brilliant marigold
        whose warm scent perfumes the skies.
The moon is a hummingbird that hovers,
        sipping nectar as it flies.

## Harmony

Friends and parties make sweet music—
        piano keys playing magic.

**Five Things to do in Waiting Rooms to get Yourself Noticed**

Just nip out to the corridor and, in a twirl or two –
        a ballerina pirouette of course – change your costume
and go save the world. Then return to your place in the queue.
        Super heroes set good examples in the waiting room.

While others check out the magazines or attempt crosswords,
        flip out that *War and Peace* you carry around to impress
on these occasions. Insert a page-mark about two-thirds
        of the way. Soon you will feel flushed with the rush of success.

Do a spot of yoga meditation – nothing tranquil –
        I'm talking headstands, bellows-breathing and breath retention.
The lion-pose – rolling eyes and tongue well out – will fulfil
        your objective of capturing everyone's attention.

Read: 'Five Things to do in Waiting Rooms to get Yourself Noticed'
        and respond without inhibition. Either read aloud
for ALL to hear, assume they are deaf and need your practised
        and boisterous laughter. Therapy, that infects a crowd.

Or at the very least, jot down your 'Five Things *not* to do.'
        It may give you perverse pleasure, but won't provide much wealth.
Or waggle your ears and twiddle your thumbs – that's restful too.
        No one can say that you neglect your own or others' health!

## Full Moon over Compton Verney

Seduced by white rock,
full moon descends, drunkenly
leaning on pine tree.

## A Fistful of Mud

A fistful of mud enters Gopal's mouth of mischief,
        but Mother Yashoda stops him from swallowing.
She peeks into a toothless grin where all cosmic space
        with suns and moons and planets is revolving.

Note: The baby Krishna was called Gopal and Yashoda was his foster mother.

## Sreeman Mishu Barua

Born in Chittagong, Bangladesh, in 1971, Mishu has studied in Bangladesh, Holland and the United Kingdom. His first collection, *Take me to your Heart*, was published in Chittagong. His work has appeared in newspapers, magazines and pamphlets, at home and abroad, including in the Writers Without Borders anthology, *The Shakespeare Memorial Room*. His collection, *My Will of Freedom* (Raka Books) has been accepted for publication in America.

## Hug

After a belligerent battle a whole day
over the madness of conquering,
calmness comes in your embrace –
I flow and rise in a joyful tide.

I walk endlessly the whole day
in each moment I burn with a single oath,
inspiration comes in your embrace –
we talk in each other's heart.

I take all the pain I get on the way,
lose in ease those which are to be lost,
forget the sorrow in your embrace –
and become replenished again.

Impoverished of self-esteem,
when I live very close to obliteration,
it is the divinity of your embrace –
makes me aware of my depravity.

To get the golden goose like others
when I become soulless and low,
it is the love in your embrace –
that saves me from the beckoning of darkness.

Often the world turns dim and cloudy,
witches laugh striking fierce thunders,
I forget to fear in your embrace –
there remains my happy days of a whole year.

**Imagination**

How boundless is the strength of imagination!
It created Satan on one side, God on the other –
human beings, who die off easily,
most unscrupulously it presented to them
the hope of immortality.

There is a place unlimited beyond limit,
where millions of wings of imagination –
full of colours –
scatter our wishes,
where satisfaction and happiness
pour into every nook and corner,
where extreme eagerness to gain
readily subdues the pain of loss,
like a cyclone it swirls fast
from one side to the other in rage
and wants to bring back to us
all that may never happen in reality.

Man doesn't realise that beyond his own limit
in the land of unending wishes,
he himself remains unfulfilled –
the more he glorifies God in imagination,
the more he himself becomes miserable.

## Caricature

What sort of master are You, O Lord?
Such a joker,
if You've given us life
why have You made death to accompany?
You've given us a heart to understand others –
instead, we deceive by always looking at ourselves.
If You've created us in Your own shape
why do our bodies get dysfunctional?
You've given us a happy home – yet
peace remains scarce.

If we are made of the same material
why is there such a difference
in colour, structure, form?
Though You gave us intelligence
we stumble at every step.
Your creation will know You –
is that what You fear?
Or else why do You send apostles
to spread Your sermons?
You've let truth and falsehood fight in our minds
and Satan dance in Your own playground.

## Leave Me

Whatever You wanted to do with us
has failed – I am sure of it.
Now leave my shadow
leave my body
leave my mind –
if You are so unearthly without a body,
Almighty, why don't You create one of Your own?
Leave my shadow
leave my body
leave my mind,
do not adhere to me
like an incurable disease,
do not possess me
like a blind, deaf and mute, mad ghost,
if You are the Almighty –
create Your own image, now,
leave my shadow
leave my body
leave my mind –
after concealing Yourself
with only some worthless lanterns to find You –
what sort of a joke is this?

## To Religious Leaders

The best for the ass is to keep quiet.
Because if it opens its mouth, besides bad breath
the peculiar sounds it will excrete
no-one in the world would be bothered by,
the ass will only fulfil the meaning of its name.
Maybe asses know the situation –
and by knowing it, except something like 'baah...'
they don't make a single sound.
Maybe that's what you didn't know.

Or though knew, you never thought
we would ever investigate that far –
nobody among us would be
so 'ridiculously insane' as to unveil your character
from analysing the words you've stated.
Whatever you thought was wrong.

I have never seen your God, why only me –
billions of people on this planet
whom you make 'God's subjects' –
not a single one of them has ever encountered Him.
They hear your recited 'holy words'
and blindly imagine with their heartfelt belief –
according to those
He must be something astounding.

I listen to your words and measure you,
as detectives re-construct a face
from the bones recovered from the grave –
the same way I analyse your character
from those of your cited 'holy words'.

## Warning

You cannot loot my freedom
to safeguard your faith,
plug both your ears if you like –
I must speak of what I understand.

Once when you preached your religion
and ruthlessly took someone out of his faith
where was this of your wisdom then?
You thought your faith was purer than his,
let me tell you now and please keep it in mind –
what I am saying is purer than your faith.

It sees a human as a human being
not as anybody's servant,
it teaches humans to be fearless,
gives total freedom of speech.

Therefore, be cautious
lest your faith's tail grow too long –
and get stamped upon while walking.

### Unconquerable

The more you want to subdue,
the more I will be rejuvenated –
for as many times you sentence to death,
a tensile chest, I will appear in front
with a thousand lives,
I will take birth in house to house
a freedom aspiring child,
I will be the thrill of victory
in each heart.

In the dialogues of the wise,
on the table of debates,
during new discoveries and inventions,
I will be the words –
I will be the heart-tremoring slogan
in every freedom-seeking revolution,
revolt and demonstration.
The more you try to obliterate my entity
the more intense will be my existence.

Each drop of my blood is a seed:
the more you shed,
I will germinate as many;
for as many times you destroy me,
I will return a new face;
the more you injure me with humiliation,
abhor, strike over strike;
the more you encage me with lies,
deception and blind faith,
the more you neglect –

I will be the blazing sun that brings a new day –
the more intensely I will glow from sky to sky.

**Shong-shoptok**

(one who knows one's defeat is inevitable, yet fights with bravery)

Mother, you're mistaken by giving me birth here.
In this country of a thousand hyenas
I am an ugly duckling – hopeless,
hiding in the bushy tall-grass, soaked in mud,
I am not safe anywhere here –
with a hungry, shivering body,
pressing my wings one over the other
waiting for nightfall.
I feel safer in the dark
though from every direction
sniffing the smells in the air,
sniffing the smells from the soil
in a joyful chore –
hyenas hunt for me.

I am waiting,
waiting to be a beautiful goose
when, observing me,
beauty would overpower their saliva
and leaving their ferocious behaviour
hyenas would become more humane.

Mother, give your blessings today
and wish the day to come
when I won't have to flee any more from
all those hyenas' shameless, bestial jaws.

**No**

When you said No to me,
my spirit was already fully glowing with passion.
I was flying within a huge pocket of thick happiness –
how flawlessly blue is the sky – from there it then seemed!
I almost believed the clouds were running along –
they are my friends,
as the greenish fields on the ground and the blue-eyed ocean.
Raged rays of the sun could only make me smiling-warm –

when suddenly came a No, slashing through my dream
deafening the silence of scenic meditation.
What does it mean?
This single word! One syllable!
How much strength could it hold altogether?
It echoed and echoed on the walls of my heart –
how very tough a word, No!
At what ease it shattered the mirrors I set
in the roots of my belief to a thousand pieces,
brought to collapse my cosmos very carefully weaved
and multiplied in seconds to a thousand Nos
savouring my very conceived existence.

Did I build my world in such a precarious state?
So that a No's one bullet
can righteously track me down,
viciously hunt me down with a haunting valour,
obliterate me from my cherished unblemished sky?
I fell against the earth hard – hopes demised –
a stopped heart – with a lungful of blood, vomiting,
still two open eyes to observe the end of the finale.

No air is needed here,
a piece of sky is not needed, a humble no to flying anymore.

This No summons the total annihilation of a being,
convokes him to take his merciless journey to the end;
this No can erase all dreams,
announce the death and relieve a soul from
ever-blissfully living—
your simple No.

Beyond focus a corpse ruptures
to release fully fledged a thousand Nos within, instantly.

**Meaning**

As shoutedly as I can I say,
Human life does not bear any extra meaning
there is nothing after death.
You disagree,
these are all assumptions.
You say,
we humans are the superior beings
there is more glory awaiting us after death.
Still these are all assumptions.

From this coast to the other
rolls a sea of assumptions
with the treasure-truth lying deep beneath.
It undulates and glitters
as if the sea itself is the treasure
and gives our life some new meaning
with its encroaching playful waves,
every now and then.

# Rubina Din

Born in Pakistan, Rubina has lived in England for almost all of her life. A qualified teacher, she works as a literacy consultant, training teachers in Birmingham and also with children in developing their writing skills. She has had two short stories published by Tindal Street Press and work aired on BBC radio.

**What is Happiness?**

I feel trapped
so caught
yanked from behind
stood in line

I feel so vague
so caught
my mind a blank
heartbeat dead

I feel so tired
so caught
escape impossible
life listless

I feel dead
caught in the grave
at last I'm happy
I am free.

**What am I Doing Here?**

What am I doing here?
My life shackled down by responsibility
the world will pass me by
death will claim me after life denied

Who am I living for?
My life bound by others around

animals whom God neglected intellect
are better off than me
they have a greater freedom
less choices to make

they know what they are doing here.

**Friendships Lost**

Each moment in time new friends
all pass through a single frame
these moments frozen in space
trapped and kept in the mind's box
no time to stop and look back
life carries on ploughing through
new and seemingly better experiences
friendships dwindle slowly as
other experiences seem more important
yet reminiscent memories remain
of times past, which were
so important then but now remain faded pictures.

Every now and again suppressed
windows open showing the life once had
the mind's melancholic mirror lets
memories flood quickly, silently dancing
across the usually closed mind
for a small silent time reminding
of times that were
but in time life's clutter closes them
until next a frozen moment unfreezes.

**Death**

Death's dark hands
entwined around your throat
merciless, shrills of laughter
leave his lips as you draw
out your final breath.

Prepare yourself –
to kiss the life you love
goodbye. No time to weep
or wail for life is gone, more
quickly than it came.

Remember life's joys
as she flashes before your eyes
like some lover without faith
she left you for some other man
and no life leaves, for death.

Despair not.
Have faith in God
the God that gave you life
he shall reward you with
life eternal when death
shall reign no more.

**Mask**

A spear through
the heart
I wake coldly
daring not to breathe
the vicious cough continues
Oh God, I say,
help him
ease his pain.

I get up mechanically
lay out the medical apparatus
my heart no longer involved
mind overtaken
medication given

my eyes full of tears
they fall in fountains
yet no one knows
the smiles continue.

## Destruction

The creation was a thing of beauty
but the destruction will far surpass it

birds will continue to sing
rabbits to burrow new homes
insects continue their natural destruction for survival

without knowledge
without understanding they continue

though the flowers continue to bud
the trees continue to leaf
the crickets continue to chirp

yet man shall be preparing
to destroy his fellow man

without pity
without shame man continues
his futile shameless destruction
against the laws of nature

what manner of insect is man
who for pleasure and power destroys?

## Who Are We?

We came in peace to earn
a living and send it back home
little did we know then
that we would become armed destroyers
of our languages and cultures.

We come as loners bedding
wherever the night would hold us
our ultimate aim always to provide
for families: parents, children, relatives back home.

In our haste, we lost our children
uncontrollable flames licked through the youth
seeds of defiance took root
blossoming into anger.

Abandoned, we are losing our future.

**What Will Tomorrow Bring?**

What will tomorrow bring?
Will it be filled with regrets
of yesterdays gone by
or wistful whisperings of
heady summer times?

Did those armies of days
in full flight neatly
march steadily by without
a whimper at the speed
of soldiers gone from the eye?

Those days have fallen into graves
buried like the dead
yet sometimes ghostly memories
from a powerful past return
as shades of times gone by.

**Dreams**

The mind is full of images
each more powerful than the last
every sleep holding residues of the day
a fistful of whispers that linger.

Morning breaks
homeward bound the winged fellows leave
to trap one in a jar is
time trapped in eternity
without release it shrivels up
the dying dream bottled screams for release.

Freedom comes to the rescue
grabbing them within its arms
together they leave for distant lands
time eludes the heavenly havens
built within nests of human psyches.

## Faith

My heart lies among the hills
for that is where he lives
each night my mind gently
drifts, like an Eastern breeze
toward the deep valleys
and tall hillsides
there my shadow meets with his
that governs the roots
of my heart.

## Saeeda Younus

Born in Pakistan, Saeeda has lived in England since 1960, intially writing in Urdu. She has had poems and articles published in *Ravi Newspaper* and short stories in *Katha*, through Writers Without Borders. Her poetry also appears in their anthology, *The Shakespeare Memorial Room* and she has had work commissioned by Birmingham Art Gallery for Women's International Day.

**The Marked Day**

He is going to sell me
He is going to sell me
He who pledged to protect me
He who took vows to love and honour me
He whom I trusted with my life
He to whom I gave myself for life
He is going to sell me.

Journeying on foot
My body is burning with fever
Heat of the sun is unbearable
Trekking through stony hills
Not a single tree in sight
Nor a shelter nor a refuge
Travelling to where
He is going to sell me
He is going to sell me
There is nothing I can do.

While trudging, looking for shade
At next turning I behold an oasis
An ancient tomb by thick tall trees
And a welcoming sweet water well
A sip of water and a little shade
Might bring my fever down
My whole body is tired.

Two men have covered their faces
They remain unknown to me
I think of my brother
The young strong and educated
One day he will find out
But that day will be too late for me

These men must have considered
The possibility of being discovered
And revenged by my brother
So they remain unknown to me.

The faceless men won't give me respite
They want to continue the journey
I sit down beside the well
They are having drink of water
I wait until they think of me
At last one of them
Brings me a bowl of fresh, cool water
I look towards my master, my husband
Begging him to let me rest
He turns away, that's his answer.

This is a tomb of saint
Who once helped many in trouble
Many still come here asking for help
I will come back to this place
As a way of expressing my thanks to God
And give charity to the poor
I pray silently, O God! save me.

I try to linger and pay respect
To the grave of the dead saint
The faceless can't stop me from that
Even the wicked have respect for the saint
Even thieves and robbers and dacoits
And courtesans and prostitutes.
They are getting anxious waiting for me
I have to leave now
But I will remember the saint

Who doesn't discriminate
Some come here to give
And some come here to take.

We come to a village
A mud house, a smiling young woman
A welcoming bed of woven jute
I wish I could rest for a short while
But this woman keeps talking
She is showing me some jewellery
And some bridal dresses
She thinks I have come willingly.

*My brother is at farm at the moment*
She informs me enthusiastically
He must be my prospective buyer
She has sent the men to meet her brother
They are preparing for tonight's feast
I have to choose my dress and jewellery
And be ready for the big night
My head is swimming
I pass out.

*25 years later*

It's a first Thursday of the lunar month
The Saint's tomb is crowded
With visitors from near and far
With the hustle and bustle of the particular day
The rich have come here prepared
To display their generosity
The beggars queuing up
To receive their share of charity
When everything comes to a standstill

A spectacle from another world
The sophisticated world
A car has just pulled up outside
And a beautiful woman is alighting
Her attire is lavish and immaculate
Her appearance is highly graceful
She has probably passed her prime
Yet years don't show on her face
She must have led a comfortable life
She approaches the tomb slowly.

She stands silently by the grave
And remembers the dire day
When she promised to return
If she ever survived the calamity
She recalls how God's help came
When she had lost all hope
Four men with their axes and bludgeons
Came to her rescue and saw her safe
To her brother's house.

When faceless men took her to that village
They never knew that her cousin
Was married there to a stout farmer
Who also had three brothers
When his wife began to scream and wail
He knew exactly what to do
Today she has come to celebrate
The birth of her grandson
By paying respect to the Saint
And by giving alms to the poor
Who stand in high expectation
And there waiting by the car
Is her handsome wealthy husband.

## Democracy

Democracy is a peacock
that has lots of ornamental feathers
but no wings to fly.

## Missing W

Adopted from an article by Zeyaul Haque (New Delhi)

When I was studying journalism at university
I was taught the five basic words of necessity.
For anyone who wanted to report news
the most essential were the five Ws.
I believe everyone who learned the rule
adhered to it after leaving the school:
WHAT-WHEN-WHERE-WHO-and-WHY

Until September the 11th
When one W was not enlisted
left out as if it never existed
Report after report was processed
but the crucial WHY was not addressed
All that hype and hoopla around terrorism
without evidence, Muslims accused of barbarism
CNN never mustered the courage to ask
WHY souls switch to such cruel tasks.

Only the BBC dared to catechise
and for that they had to apologise.

## Song

inspired by a Punjabi folk song

My house is two storey
and beside runs a shimmering river.
Come to me in the guise of a kingfisher
for I am a fish of five rivers.
O beloved!
Where did you spend the night of shame?
My aching heart is yet willing
to acquit you of blame.

My house is two storey
and beside runs a sparkling river.
I am still waiting for your return.
All my friends are with their lovers.
O beloved!
Where have you been last night?
How could you rest away from me
and not think of my plight?

My house is two storey
and beside is a beautiful region
where swings are hung tall in trees
and lovers unite in rainy season.
O beloved!
Monsoon have come and gone too soon,
the flower bud of heart's desire
is forever seeking to bloom.

My house is two storey
and beside is a luscious orchard.
When scent of lemon blossoms fills the air
young girls come to sing a ballad.
O beloved!
Delights of life are not for me
and remember that still waiting for us
is a swing on a mango tree.

## Free Woman

I am a free woman of this
modern day and age.
I have broken free from chains
and also from a cage.

I was not allowed to speak in church
and was deemed inferior.
In no way I could express myself
and that gave me hysteria.

Putting pen on paper was not permitted
that I couldn't plan
because no one but the man was the pen
and the pen was the man.

The only privilege that I enjoyed
was once in my life.
The only time to make the decision
who will make me a wife.

While chances were few and saying no
just to please myself
could mean that I was in danger of
being left on the shelf.

So I often said yes to pick myself
a life of harmony.
Manacled I was for life afterwards
submitted to the tyranny.

I am a free woman now and a man
is a game for me.
I can love him and cherish him and
make him bend his knee.

Since I was thirteen I chased my man
for many a year
all through the college too I couldn't,
from his way, keep clear.

At last I managed to ensnare him
and quickly was engaged.
Then I pushed him for an early marriage
although he wasn't prepared.

But I had all the answers, mainly that
we do love each other.
We'll help each other to build for us
a rosy future together.

I said not to worry for he had many
doubts about the matter.
At last I managed to make him think that
all was for the better.

I was married to him yesterday
and I'm divorced today.
The strain of marriage was too much
for me to take in any way.

What kind of husband is he who
can't even cook for me?
To do housework and be compliant
is not my cup of tea.

I can cook and clean when I feel like it
but why should I do?
I have got a better job and I earn much more
then he can ever do.

It's easy to have a takeaway every day
as long as I don't pay.
If it suits him he can live with me
or he can go away.

I can use him and abuse him and
ruin him any day.
The things he used to do to me
I can do to him today.

**The Good Old Days**

They were the good old days
what a good thing it was the modern technology.
When father and son and mother and daughter
could all join in to watch TV
when warming up in a TV lounge at the end of the day
it united the family.

Then came forty channels
and everybody liked what they offered in terms of diversity.
Now father has his own TV in his own bedroom
so that out of variety
he can watch by himself his preferred movie channel
not befitting to watch with the family.

Even so, observe in contemplation
the Germans and the French are much more forward
when offering adults entertainment.
Us in Britain cannot compete with them in this sort of attainment.
Late night shows are not for kids but they can be temptations –
beware! There is a need for restraint.

They were the good old days
when mother and father and son and daughter
all joined in to watch TV
now all of them in their own bedrooms
have everything of the necessity
telephones, videos, computers, TVs and at the end of the day
everyone retires to their own luxury.

## The Pledge

I will be a loyal and faithful spouse to you.
All I ask for in return is your trust in me.

I make this day a solemn promise to you:
to be unfaithful is unthinkable that I shan't be.

The knowledge that you never doubt my love for you
gives me strength when you are away from me.

Passions don't last forever and that is true
but fidelity lasts a lifetime and chaste I shall be.

My passionate love is forever reserved for you
to be chaste is easy now until you can come to me.

Faith and trust and passion and purity too:
four elements are a must for love between you and me.

## Rajni Roy

Born in Tanzania, Rajni was educated in England, at Hull University and at Lincoln's Inn. After a career as a barrister, he taught at the University of Central England, as a Principal Lecturer in Law. He has since retired. His poetry been published by The Cannon Poets and recited on BBC radio on a number of occasions.

## Roots

Family Tree

My roots run deep
are scattered and run wide
my grandfather is
Indian by descent
African by birth
British by choice.

His grandfather was
Indian with no choice
but proud shipping ancestry.
My grandma is
Anglo-Saxon stock
and her parents were the same.

Citizen of the global village,
I represent tomorrow.
They say man
has not changed in aeons;
will I, my dad, my granddad
make any difference?

I don't know
maybe
you don't know
does anybody know?
Nobody knows
does anybody care?

## Love has Many Faces

A pack of fifty-two cards has but four aces,
but love, whether you love or are being loved, has many faces.
  A diamond has the usual sixty-four or more facets,
  but when you unfold love you see its many facets.
So walk with me love and take a few paces
as we examine your many faces.

First, love is caring, caring for someone more than yourself.
Love is sharing too with many or few.
Then love is giving and not expecting a return
  as you would in a business because otherwise loving is no fun
and yet true love like the bread cast upon the water returns to you manifold,
  for true love multiplies and true love grows, if truly given as it unfolds.
Love is never a cheap bargain because the only price for love is love,
  but it is a fair and just bargain once you pay the price with love.
Use not a plastic credit card for love
  for plastic card buys only plastic love.
Love is fun, love is joy, but it's no one's puppet or toy.
Love can cause you worry and stress, or agony and pain
  and, mishandled, can lead to hate, vengeance or shame.
Love and hate are two opposite emotions
  and the two are the two sides of the same coin,
  so flip not the coin of love.

With its many faces love is a plethora of emotions in Panavision-Technicolor
and yet it can be summed up in one encyclopaedic, all-embracing word:
  UNDERSTANDING
and when you have understanding you have everything,
as love is at home and a permanent resident in understanding.

## Imagine

If there was no sun
there will be no moon
no lunatics
no romantics.

## Angel Sleeps

Little angel Dominic sleeps.
Only two, but travelled far and wide,
from home, Dubai, to home, England,
from mum to Nani and granddad.

His mum is stressed, dad double-stressed.
Their name is Cope, but they can't cope.
Nani can cope with the Copes.
Angel sleeps after play and sleeps.

Adults act their dramatic parts out,
each trying to avoid being called 'Out!'
Baby is affected, is a major stake,
but none dare disturb his sleep, or awake
blessed, guarded angel sleeps and sleeps.

**"When love returns how little of love**
**even the lover understands"**

A heart is never truly broken
it only seems to be
when grief and disappointment
have struck it cruelly.

The pieces soon come together,
time eases the distress
and one day you feel whole again
at peace content to rest.

Hearts do mend
eventually stronger for the stroke
loving and more gentle
than before they broke.

Like the restoration
on a shattered bowl,
Life, the renovator, resurrects
the devastated soul.

## Life is no Video

Our life is a varied mixture of bliss and
unhappiness, a pentathlon
born alone we live with family and friends
but we go empty-handed alone.
Life is a one-way transit passageway
with its stops and starts but no reply.
You can't bring back or relive the magic moments
of past happiness.
Nor can you change, edit or erase a tiny bit of your distress.

Life is the most precious gift of God, you take it or leave it
be happy and grateful whilst you can, for there is no repeat.
Sin and wrong if you will and even keep it a secret
but make no mistake, God's book-keeping is perfect
and you take a certain chance that in the end you will lose
for karma will catch up with you and not accept any excuse.

Do unto others or give them what you want from them.
Life is no video.
If you need love you must give love
for the grace in love is not in taking but in giving love.
If you want joy, tranquillity and peace
don't aggravate others but try to please.
Fun fills life's cup of happiness and makes it worth living
and there is a lot of fun and joy in giving.

There are myriads alive in the universe, but each
life is but a cameo
and your only life is no video.
There is no pressing forward to live a future
moment now, no retake, no editing,
no replay, erase or even regretting!
If life is a video, it is His video.

**Life's Crutches**

*Parkdrive*
You are keeping me alive
every disaster I reach for a fag
very soothing after the first drag.

*Prozac*
You are my friend indeed
when depression strikes it's you I need
you pick me up, you let me slip again.
Your side-effects I have yet to suffer,
until then please be my buffer.

*Alcohol*
I am not addicted or dependent on liquor
it just helps me feel my sorrows are lighter
raises my nervous spirit to feel free
it tears my mask so all can see the real me.

**Burst of British Summer**

England is a land of seasons
not gradual, but
sudden change of season:
like I first had four decades ago.

In March, sailing from France
I had mist, rain and sun in Paris,
strong wind, waves, hailstones and
snow in the Channel
and brilliant sunshine
at Victoria station
all in a day!

John Smith, the British Council
Representative who came
to receive me, an overseas student,
said with a smile,
"Hello and welcome
to our typical British weather!"

Things haven't changed:
last week we had rain, wind
with hailstones as big as marbles
and a burst of summer sunshine
all in an afternoon.

Long live British weather!
Cool Britannia,
make the best of it
and enjoy roses whilst they bloom.

## Diwali

Hindu festival of Diwali is a comprehensive festival:
it takes in Thanksgiving for return of Lord Rama
to his rightful throne; triumph of good over evil
and the start of Ramrajya; utopia
with fireworks and deepavali lights.

Diwali echoes British Harvest Festival,
Guy Fawkes 5th Nov. and Christmas all rolled into one.
How appropriate that we now have
multicultural multi-faith multi-ethnic community in Britain
which in harmony celebrates our varied customs.

So roll on the Christian millennium.
We are ready,
if you are ready for us.
Diversity and unity of purpose is our strength
and for this, we the new British, give thanks.

**Serenity**

is what is left
when stress has done
its worst and lost.

When difficulties
are faced head on,
when mind triumphs
over life's real stresses:

changing things we can
and accepting things we cannot.

The difference
between the two
ushers the dawn
of lasting peace, serenity.

**Union**

All I heard were three explosions.
I crawled from my car
got on my feet
and started walking down what was once Derry Street.

As the dust cleared
the sound stopped
deafening my ears:
it seemed like years.
I felt the tears running down my face
as I walked away from the place.

I seemed to remember,
ten minutes ago,
there were houses
and shops
and mothers with children
running around their feet.

Roman Catholic, Protestants too,
all going about their business,
all had a lot to do.
I heard someone shouting
about a body they had found.

Now all I could hear
were their cries
as another one died.
I walked on and saw
another pair of feet
that moments before
walked down the street.

So Ireland is at last
United in this street.

## Amina Shelly

Amina was born in Sylhet, Bangladesh and has lived in the UK since 1989. Her poetry was first collected in *The Bangla Journal,* in Canada. She has had poems translated into Bengali and published in *Nandan*, Dhaka and a short story in *Whispers in the Walls*, published by Tindal Street Press.

## Foreword

*The mind is of greater measures*
*the flesh five feet two*
*the voice—wise as the ageing world*
*Hai! Only one language to bring it true!*

**"I was born where singing for women is against the odds"**

Gone are just a few young days. Yet there's enough to fill library shelves beyond your height. Would you be surprised if I told you—I am a movie by day and a novel by night?

For forty years long I speak of life. You read your prayers, ignore me on the way to the mosque. I wonder if I had all the wrong things all along, or is this your way of saying, 'that is your way and this is mine'? I wonder!

Forty years more I paint and draw. You can clean your comb with my brushes. I see it all—my sketchbooks are scrap paper, packing material. You make me believe I matter for as long as I am here. As soon as I go, all will go. Like the current. Like the river.

For another forty years I take pictures in colour. When you shred photos of my friends who pass away, it's as though you erase my childhood. I still love you. Keep you in my heart live and vivid. Tell me then, when you tire from the ties of this world, would you shred my heart? Would you take it with you?

Forty years thence I sound a verse. You're still drunk in your prayers, your crops, your pets and ponds. You love me most and understand more, yet why? A dose of paan or a tap on the shoulder is all I can ask for. Apparent contentment; is that what I wear letting a sigh deep inside—will I ever reach the streams you travel? Feel the strengths you never reveal?

**Remembering Nanji**

She couldn't see. She'd touch and caress me, feel my face, hair, ears and hands, and that was enough to love me.

The pale light of my table lamp makes pictures in the dim night—you dress me in a sheathing of care where dusk and dawn unite.

In the warmth of your touch I see the water that links Surma to the Bay of Bengal. Sometimes I ache in the fire of my own memories. Then again, my bones are wrapped in tiny threads called heal.

Snow falls as if thousands of glow worms scratching their backs on my window. When morning is December the picture prolongs, although I know the night is no more.

## On Foreign Streets

In the heart of this kingdom daffodils blossom. Daffodils rot away inside this kingdom. Aprils rise here all year through. All year round Aprils fall. Darkness settles and hounds quarrel. Here in the land of concrete greyness sleepless nights stretch to miles.

I know the lights that are yet to be lit, the rays that hide beneath the surface of watching the openness through closed doors. Earthen age too, rotting the years away. They look at me as though I am a foreigner on foreign streets? For whom the day is many decades. Strange is everything, everywhere.

## The Silent Diary

*I*

Why do you call me
black, brown, asian, muslim, bengali
british this, british that,
sometimes in general, ethnic minority.

Why do songs of Jamuna
assume the river to be feminine?
Is it because it's an Asian river
rising in anger
hurt the way my mother had been?

They fall for the sea
these rivers can't stand and look within.
You can yet don't and so the assumption
am I not my own person
and Bangla – the colour of my skin.

*II*

The telephone rings and I let you go
for an hour or so we drift apart
you in a world of your liking
as I turn towards my own heart.

How we say –
nothing could ever come between the two
yet somehow something does
though for a small part of life
the telefax rings to separate us.

*III*

To earth I ask of earth
to the air of nothing but air
as kingfishers urge the fishful sea
I ask water – water me.

Pleased is the mind
that each time I open my eyes and see
from each chapter of the day
takes with care what little I find.

*IV*

You come as early as 4:00am
you come as early as 4:00pm.

With all my heart I worship your energy
and you now watch over my head
spread unbearable heat throughout this body.

You come as harsh as 4:00am
Dear sun, you come as harsh as 4:00pm.

*V*

Every other day a little unhappiness
every now and then a little unwellness
how about you?

There are times when we're bedewed,
every other while a fire –
the inside burns as though a flame
plays its charm on liquor.

You know what's in your heart
for that is your own.
As for what is mine –
I am doing alright
except every now and again.

*VI*

Evening dew
your affection touches the soul.

Though what I suffer
is no pain, yet for some
this is a mild term
with hands on heart, the mind sincere
I wish them eternal joy
the songs that are born
in the silent diary
                                        and die therein.
Peace be upon them. Amen.

**When I am Seven**

The country is a hayfield when I am seven.

I am mobbed by dusky air, embers sizzling in the west. Candles light up the shadows of tulshi. Azan hits me ear to ear. Dancing in the forecourt are the chicks I most admire. As the ducklings play hide and seek in this festive hour, my spare time enjoys the scent of marigolds.

When I am only seven I have a country of playing fields.

## Kalpana Ganguly

Kalpana was born in Kenya and brought up in Uganda, before settling in England. In East Africa she worked as a teacher and amateur actor. She is now a civil servant and is involved in a variety of voluntary work. Her poetry has been published by Writers Without Borders.

**Home Is...**

East or West they say
'home is best'.
When I went to Rome
it brought memories home
of yesteryears
standing in St. Peter's Square
I saw the grandeur
as splendid as that of the
Golden Temple of Amritsar
breathtaking beauty
of Niagara Falls
the incomparable Victoria Falls
yet there can be no comparison
each awe inspiring vision
gives equal pleasure.
The splendour of the Taj Mahal
and glory of St. Paul's Cathedral
giving equal pride to architecture.
In majestic Himalayas I see
the captivating beauty of Kilimanjaro
seeing Ben Nevis gives me the same thrill –

*foetus killing in India,*
*abandoning babies in*
*'living graves' in China –*

Pure and holy are
the waters of Avon
same as Ganges and Yamuna.
Why the boundaries
then of yours and mine?
When I am gone
rest me on the banks of Avon
for home is where
the heart is.

## Sapan Vihar

*1. Pine-Ache*

From Viking Land
came to reside a little angel
in this abode of dreams with colour of love
she painted one more dream
surrounded by evergreen.
Now my little Tonje and Sapan Vihar
pine for each other.

*2. Foreign Affair*

Language of love is universal
yet my Anna
had to find words in a dictionary
and her father laid rules
for his daughter: NO LOVERS.
Alas my dream of universal love and universal family
lay shattered in father's diktats
and Anna's dictionary.

## Milan Disappears

Summer of nineteen eighty three
on arrival at the chalet
within minutes who but Milan
managed to lock himself in the bathroom
amongst mum's panic attacks
and little one's screams and shouts.
Daddy managed to get him out.

Summer of nineteen eighty four
on the sandy beaches of Cornwall
wind swept away our Milan's beach ball.
Mum consoled him with ice-cream
saying never you mind
it's only the ball that has gone.

Summer of nineteen eighty five
we were at Bournemouth fair
watching roller coasters and children eating candy floss
suddenly mum noticed
Milan was nowhere to be seen.
Daddy said stay calm
we shall find our cherub.
Mummy holding her little one
Daddy holding Sapan
went in opposite directions.
Mum was now exhausted and about to collapse
when lo and behold! she saw
right in the middle of the fairground
her little darling holding his lollipop.
Mum's heart sank with relief.

Running towards her little tearaway
she said – If ever again you disappear
I promise I shall make you invisible!

**No Postcard from Botswana**

Reporter on TV
painting South African streets red
A mother in Sutton
awaiting a postcard from Botswana, Cape Town
anxiously dialling mobile numbers –
destination switched off –
frantically praying for the safety of traveller son
no postcard from Botswana
but a call from Wylde Green
no not from traveller son – from resident son
mugged at knife-point
relieved of his cash at a cash point
no reporter there painting streets of Sutton red
no candid cameras to capture the moment.
Now the call from traveller son
Hello mum – it was great cool
trouble there? What trouble?
From unsafe South Africa to safe Sutton.

## Designer Age

Designer babies, designer parents
we live in designer age
gay and lesbians will wedlock
we live in nineties not in dark ages
as you know this is designer age
why conceive unexpectedly
when designer way is test-tube baby
why go through labour pain
when surrogate motherhood can be norm
whether sixteen or sixty
you can have a baby unaided by man
this is called DIY creation.
Is this a blessing or a curse
in this designer age?

**Waiting**

I am waiting for the bus
let me finish the make-up
Oh! dear mirror seems too small
and I miss my bus –
While I am waiting for the next one
let me finish the make-up
can't find right colour lipstick
as I look up
next bus passes by –
Trying to look presentable
I am surely going to miss the boat.
Waiting, waiting, always waiting…

## Christmas Wish

Silent night, starry night
Chimney is inviting.
Be my Father Christmas
and fill up my stocking –
be my little elf
and let me be the fairy.

## The Hook

The moments spent with you
yet the singing brook flowed –
the trout in the river
seemed to have similar fate as mine
where an angler catches it
not for keeps but for fun.

## Colour Blind

Colour my world with red
not with dread
Colour my world with white
and fill it with light
Colour my world with orange bright
and not with grey
Colour my world with black
and let there be contrast
Colour my world with the colours of rainbow
and let me be colour blind.

## Common Goal

My love wants red roses
I have grown primroses
My love wants tulips
I have grown cowslips
Isn't this our paradise?
Contrast is the spice of life.

## West is East

Forever reaching out
from East to West
branches to meet
beyond the roots
seemingly touch
on the horizon.

## Cannon Hill Park

Woods and colourful trees
ducks in the pond
joggers and ambling walkers
bikers too –

apart from a little coot
no birds in sight

picnic tables –
                    here and there
benches in memory of
actors and film directors
          some poets too

but apart from a coot
no birds in sight
the rightful residents
of the woods.

## Kampta Karran

Kampta was born in Guyana on the South American continent and is a Research Fellow at the University of Warwick, in The Centre for Race and Ethnic Relations. As well as publishing in Sociology, he has co-edited and had work appear in *The Shakespeare Memorial Room* by Writers Without Borders and *The Griot.*

**Trees**

See Me
Please

Dear trees

This is your friend
Your ward
Greetings!

Your leaves
have seen
my deepest secret
your shades
have shared
my joys
my sorrows
your roots
are watered
by my tears
your existence
has chronicled
my histories
through the years.

Trees
You know me
as I am
the causes
the effects
my limitations
my fears
my aspirations
your shades
hold records
of my pains
my labours
beneath your shadows
are buried my treasures.

## Trees

You bowed
your branches
in respect
you shed
your leaves
to mark
my sorrows
you whispered
soothingly
to banish
my woes.

Why trees?
Why shelter me
clothing me
with your naked self?
I like you
am fixed
by laws
unlike you
I'm not allowed
to bloom
though withered
must live
a spectacle
and to you
blind naked
indifferent you
I am
a helpless ward
worming in your shadows
praying for death
yet desiring to live
to enjoy
your blossom
your fragrance
your shade.

Yes trees

I live at your roots
for I am rootless
from you
I draw strength and solace
denied me
by the world of humans.

And one day trees

I'll be
cut and burned
when your seeds
spring up
mine will
be no more.

Perennial trees

Shelter me
soon your shadows
will be empty
you will be meaningless
no wards
no secrets

Sentinel Trees

Nothing Trees

Forever Trees.

**Cyclism**

They claimed a two-wheeled cycle
Of course on our behalf
They promised us a miracle
They nailed us to the cross.

This was a champion cycle
Complete with gears and brass
The bells rang pure
The brakes held stiff
With riders strong and fast.

This is the thing you fought for
For which your fore-parents died
As the heirs apparent
You must be satisfied!

They promised and gave us hard work
Punctuated with little rest
You're never to ride this cycle
And those who tried are dead!

The cycle is well guarded
Peddled East and West
Riders, guards, managers
Enjoying its very best.

They ride at their pleasure
All the prizes covet
The path the front wheel takes
The back knows seldom of it.

Each rider chooses his own gear
Charting his course to follow
If it suits his fancy
He sells a spoke also.

Under this cyclism
Our bicycle gradually declined
The wheels got old
The gears are gone
The bells are hoarse and sticking
The brakes are cut
The brass profaned
The chains un-oiled and croaking.

The riders are no longer keen
The seat is worn and thin
The managers confused
Hoping to loan that which they claimed
To those from whom they claimed it.

Meanwhile the guards contemplating
Their newly found Anthem
And terror take ova, take ova the whole a foreva
Bim!
Be dim.

At the cycle repair shop
The artisans are discussing
The wheels and types of revolution
The handle and direction
The bearings and endurance
The opposition and the cyclical situation

The bike is museum material
Food for posterity
We are hungry
We demand the worker's fare.

No! No!
You're the owners
Must be responsible and austere
Soon we'll be riding
Through the open and the clear.

They've long since killed
Our two-wheeled cycle
Now intent on riding us
The same to replace
Else we'll end up
Un-martyred
Yet nailed to the cross.

## Saffron Tea

You sit in
accustomed permanence
rose cultured oysters digested.

They wake
to dry dis-inheritance
thorn-wrapped perennial infected.

## U'iou Theou

He sat
upon his created ass
the masses waved clothes and branches.

They nailed
him to their stolen cross
salvation sings redemption dances.

Note: The title, U'iou Theou, is Greek for Son of God. The poem was named by my friend and brother Ben Franklin Culbertson.

**Behold!**

Ant & Bee
retreat confront
surviving thr'u' shared industry.

Spiders on
their vocation mount
that silkened thread of tyranny.

**In Transit**

The jaa-haa-gin
came on ships of old
to build new bharat desh.

Now coolies
with their feet do vote
to God's own blessed place.

## Sail bye

Driftwood
has no station
save water and waves for company.

Roots
dead! branches gone
just roaming upon the sea.

## Sapna Vihar

The wise ones
carriage camelled to source
good food and pleasant company

Tota Mina's
coded discourse
of songs of love of poetry.

**Fite Man**

Vasu dewa kut am ba kam
Wuk man pickney get dam vex
Otha people a inherit dem parents sweat
Dis a hut dem bad bad bad
Dem throw back an punda and dem get mad
Vasu dewa kut am ba kam

How lang wuk man gat fu mine
De ole haigue pickney of pantomine
Wuk man wuk dem wuk an dem plan
Wuk man pickney tun fite man
Wid cut-lass shap-een all two side
Dem sid down a dem doe mouth
To guard dem pride
Vasu dewa kut am ba kam

Fite man vision plain as day
Unity an justice de only way
Arjuna, Joshua and Jihad
Fire pan babee lan
Bun dem Gad
Vasu dewa kut am ba kam

Wuk man pickney in de street
Solida buss dem head an bruk dem feet
Wid two argans gane dem na give up
Liberation lies in dem arm an dem gut
Vasu dewa kut am ba kam

Wuk man pickney gut in arm
Ole haigue scream in great alarm
Bitta bullet scramble knat
Ole higue dead crass fight man lap
Vasu dewa kut am ba kam

Note: 'Vasu dewa kut am ba kam' means 'The universe is one family.'